TURNING
TURNOVER
AROUND

Thanks for keeping the noise level down and the sales up.

John Maly, President, Maly's LLC (2007)

I can't imagine where we would be without your leadership and direction.

John Maly, President, Maly's LLC (2000)

Mark's greatest strengths include fairness, loyalty, and dedication.

Sheryl Kopp, Director of Process Improvement, Packard Bell (1993)

I have been working with Mark Vonrhein for the past six years and have found him to be loyal, hard working, and trustworthy.

Reuben Sussman, Producers Group International USA (1991)

Mark Vonrhein has been a trusted and hard-working Customer Service Manager ... for the past six years.

Hal Sazzmann, Personnel Director, Reliable Company (1991)

Congratulations for having been recommended by your manager as one of the people that he feels has potential.

Bob Grebe, Regional Director, ITT Life Insurance Corporation (1984)

Mark Vonrhein has one quality which I believe will carry him far in business ... He has integrity.

Joseph B. Rubich, General Manager, Victoria Station (1982)

TURNING TURNOVER AROUND

A 5-Step Performance
Compensation Program

Mark H. Vonrhein

iUniverse, Inc.
New York Bloomington

Turning Turnover Around
A 5-Step Performance Compensation Program

iUniverse books may be ordered through booksellers or by contacting:

iUniverse
1663 Liberty Drive
Bloomington, IN 47403
www.iuniverse.com
1-800-Authors (1-800-288-4677)

Because of the dynamic nature of the Internet, any Web addresses or links contained in this book may have changed since publication and may no longer be valid. The views expressed in this work are solely those of the author and do not necessarily reflect the views of the publisher, and the publisher hereby disclaims any responsibility for them.

ISBN: 978-0-595-50874-7 (sc)
ISBN: 978-0-595-61682-4 (ebk)

Printed in the United States of America

iUniverse rev. date: 02/16/2009

Contents

Acknowledgments

Thank you to my wife for her love, patience, and devotion.

Thank you to my sons who give me hope for the future.

Thank you to my parents who gave me an appreciation for all this country has to offer.

Thank you to my brothers and sister for accepting one another as we are.

Thank you to all my friends for their support.

Thank you to all the supervisors, managers, directors, and owners I've worked for.

Thank you to all the business trainers I've had the privilege of learning from.

Thank you to all the employees who have worked for me.

Special thanks to John Maly, Colin Walsh, Dottie Lanham, Brian Berent, Nancy Crone, and Melanie Hicken.

Preface

Demand is high for entry-level employees in the service industry, and these positions make up a large segment of a company's labor force. These employees are the face and voice of a company because they have the most contact with customers—answering questions, taking orders, selling products and services, or resolving issues. Retention of these frontline employees creates a solid foundation from which companies can carry out their strategies and initiatives. I've worked in retail, restaurants, sales, manufacturing, and distribution. I've found that whether they're retail clerks, waiters, salesman, factory workers, office staff, or telephone representatives, all entry-level employees are motivated by money and advancement opportunities. For more than a dozen years, I've used the 5-Step Performance Compensation Program to attract, motivate, and retain employees.

I've promoted the 5-Step Performance Compensation Program with all the benefits it has to offer to my colleagues where I've worked. The usual reception I received was skepticism at best. I couldn't blame them for questioning a program that's not taught in business schools and sounds counterintuitive. How can issuing employees numerous pay adjustments actually reduce payroll costs? Many executives think it sounds like "crazy talk," but what's *really* crazy is spending so much time and money training employees just to lose them to your competition for $.50 or $1.00 an hour. Some Fortune 500 companies like Cingular, RxAmerica, and Interstate Battery already use a performance compensation program to motivate and retain their employees.

Some employee turnover is part of our upwardly mobile society. Each career change provides valuable learning experiences and professional growth opportunities. Careers usually begin in entry or mid-level positions and take several turns along the way. While most managers and executives didn't start their careers in the mailroom, they've all held some interim jobs prior to their current position. Their ambition and aspirations motivated them to try their best in every position they've held. Their supervisors could see the potential of these future leaders based on their ability. Their performance made them model employees who were headed for bigger and better things in their careers.

My career had humble beginnings, and I've been fortunate to work for a number of companies who achieved exceptional growth. My entire career has been spent working directly with customers in a variety of industries. I have interacted with thousands of customers, either face-to-face or by telephone.

I spent my first seven years working at a family-owned liquor store. This high-volume retail environment exposed me to several valuable areas of business including customer service, merchandizing, marketing, and inventory control. At that time, customer service was the one thing that separated us from our competition due to the Fair Trade liquor laws that regulated alcoholic beverage prices. I noticed customers didn't mind paying a little extra for their non-alcoholic items like milk, bread, and soda when the service was fast and friendly.

My next seven years were spent at a national restaurant chain. Victoria Station was a railroad car theme restaurant that specialized in prime rib. Victoria Station became a case study at the Harvard School of Business for its ten-year expansion from one to 115 locations. It was the first in the industry to introduce standardized audio-visual training, employee benefits, and point-of-sale technology. Turnover was very low and positions were hard to come by. I worked my way through college as a waiter there and was promoted to management after graduation. This gave me experience in inventory control, cost of goods, and profit-and-loss statements.

I spent the next two years at Capital Planning Associates. This was a 100 percent commission job selling term life insurance with annuity and disability riders. An executive once explained our benefits by saying, "We have the best health insurance there is. If you don't work, you don't get paid." The office manager was one of the best motivational speakers

I've ever met. He promoted me to service manager and I trained all new recruits for the state life insurance test and their sales presentation. We showed customers the need to save money, created a sense of urgency, and offered our product as a solution. We ended that year with the second highest production out of sixty offices nationwide. This experience made me realize how hard it is to sell an intangible product and how hard employees will work without a guaranteed salary.

My next seven years were at a Maytag coin-operated laundry distributor called Reliable Company. The owner wanted the best equipment and service in the industry. This proved to be a successful strategy as the company grew from operating two machines to 50,000. The company was so successful, it was sold in a 100 percent leveraged buyout after thirty years. My first position was installation coordinator for apartments, hotels, and Laundromats. I purchased a million dollars a year in new equipment in coordination with our in-house remanufacturing operation. I was promoted to customer service manager where I renegotiated long-term tenant leases and represented the company in Small Claims and Municipal courts.

I spent the next seven years at a computer manufacturer. Packard Bell pioneered the mass merchandising of personal computers. To meet the demands of retailers, it created twenty-four-hour-a-day technical support, onsite service repairs, and multimedia point-of-purchase presentations. The strategy was to deliver cutting edge technology at the lowest price. We took market share away from our larger competitors with our willingness to launch hardware and software months before the rest. Packard Bell also became a Harvard School of Business case study for its ten-year sales growth from $800 million to $13 billion. Production capacity expanded from 50,000 units per month to 30,000 units per day while employment rose from 800 to 8,000 employees. It was an exciting time to be in the industry as the Internet was growing in popularity and multimedia technologies were being introduced.

At Packard Bell, I was part of an out-of-state call center relocation team of managers. Our three-month transition plan was thrown out the window after the 1994 Northridge, California, earthquake red-tagged four out of five buildings the company occupied. At that moment, all we had was a site selection, so leases were quickly signed and construction began immediately. Temporary operations were conducted at a nearby vacant daycare center with power and telephone lines running down the sidewalk from the construction site. We utilized the local job services facilities to recruit and interview applicants. Our first three training classes were held in a conference room, and our only training tool was a dry erase board. From these meager beginnings, the call center grew to 950 workstations with 1,750 employees operating twenty-four hours a day, 365 days a year.

My customer service team revamped processes, policies, and procedures for numerous programs. We interfaced with three onsite repair providers and a thousand service centers nationwide. We created a Pay Grade Promotion Program that increased productivity 15 percent and reduced turnover to 15 percent. Our customer service team grew to 300 agents, and my colleagues managed the higher-level functions while I had responsibility for the largest group of Level I employees.

Packard Bell made two large acquisitions that were very different from the consumer market it had pioneered. The first, Zenith Data Systems, targeted the government sector; the other, NEC North America, targeted the business sector. In both cases, the decision was made to create separate customer service groups to satisfy the unique contract requirements. We were asked to provide thirty of our best agents for the first, and sixty for the second. Imagine losing 10 percent and then 20 percent of your best employees in a week. All we could do was get busy recruiting, hiring, training, and motivating their replacements. Over a four-year period, I hired 700 entry-level employees and transferred 200 to various departments. Those were some of the most challenging and rewarding times of my career.

I spent the next eight years at a beauty supply distributor called Maly's. This was a thirty-year-old family-run business with the goal of being the best in the industry. We upgraded order entry and telephone systems to accommodate a dozen companies we acquired. Sales revenue grew 500 percent in eight years, and the company was acquired by L'Oreal Professional USA. I was fortunate to work directly for the owner who understood my program and was willing to let me use it in my customer service group when I started. Our store operations had a hundred locations and were expanding by 10 percent per year. High turnover was making it difficult to meet the demand for additional store and regional managers. I told the owner I thought my program would help reduce turnover. He said he was thinking the same thing and that it was time to try something new. Our director of store operations was well read and knew all the best retail practices. I believed the only reason the director wasn't already using this type of program was because he had never read a book about it.

Over the past fifteen years, I've hired 900 entry-level employees and encouraged the internal transfer of 270, or 30 percent of those employees. While I've supported my staff's development and advancement, I wouldn't be telling the truth if I said it doesn't hurt to lose your best employees. The only thing that hurts more is losing your best employees to your competition. I'm proud of these employees and their accomplishments. Even though all of them started in entry-level positions, many have gone on to become leads, supervisors, managers, or directors in a variety of companies. Some might say I really know how to pick them. What I say is, "I only gave them a chance, showed them a formula for success, and rewarded their performance." Their success was due primarily to their own hard work.

The accumulation of my experiences has given me a unique perspective on the value of the customer and the employees who serve them. I've become a customer service retention specialist and I wrote this book to help companies reduce their employee turnover.

Introduction

Turning Turnover Around presents a 5-Step Performance Compensation Program designed to retain employees while increasing productivity and improving the bottom line. One of the most common reasons for turnover is related to job dissatisfaction. Employees leave despite liking the company and its products, services, co-workers, and management. Their dissatisfaction is primarily due to their compensation, which is important because many employees are working from paycheck to paycheck. If employees see no relationship between their pay and their performance, they usually leave for better opportunities or more money.

Our fast-paced world has created instant coffee and instant breakfast—all you need to do is just add water. Our busy schedules make us look for quick solutions to the numerous challenges we face every day in our personal and professional lives. Unfortunately, there are no magic bullets that give instant solutions for major challenges. Most professionals avoid quick-fix programs because they don't deliver on their promises or have lasting results. The 5-Step Performance Compensation Program doesn't promise to solve all your employee issues overnight; however, it will provide you with an effective way to reduce employee turnover and increase productivity on an ongoing basis.

This book outlines the six goals all companies share and the challenges created by high employee turnover. You will discover how and why implementing the 5-Step Performance Compensation Program will not only reduce employee turnover, but also save your company money and increase productivity—thereby helping you achieve your company goals. The 5-Step Performance Compensation Program will change your relationship with your employees and turn your turnover around.

Chapter 1

Employee Turnover

Numerous studies, articles, and books explain the reasons, percentages, and costs of employee turnover, and many also offer solutions. Despite all the information available, employee turnover continues to challenge many companies. This explains why we see new books on the subject published year after year.

Costs, Rates, and Causes of Employee Turnover

Turnover costs vary from one industry, company, and position to another. The replacement cost includes recruiting, interviewing, screening, training, and payroll. These costs can range from hundreds to several thousand dollars depending on the position and training required.[1] Low productivity during the first three months of training is an additional hidden cost of employee turnover.

> **Formula for Calculating Your Annual Turnover Costs**
> Number of Employees x Turnover Rate x Hiring Costs = Turnover Cost
>
> For example: 100 employees x 30% x $1,000 = $30,000

---

[1]   Rich Williams, "Reducing Employee Turnover to Protect the Bottom Line," *San Fernando Valley Business Journal* (September 15, 2003).

Employee turnover percentages also vary from one industry, company, and position to another. These percentages range from 20 percent to 60 percent and can seem like a revolving door of new employees.[2] From my own experience, the highest turnover rates are in the lowest paying positions.

Some employee turnover is unavoidable due to graduation, promotion, relocation, and mortality. These reasons account for only a portion of your turnover rate. Job dissatisfaction is a primary reason cited in employee exit interviews. I've found the main cause of job dissatisfaction with entry-level employees is low wages. The 5-Step Performance Compensation Program is designed to address this issue.

How Employee Turnover Affects Everyone Involved

Whether you're a customer, employee, supervisor, trainer, human resources specialist, financial officer, or stockholder, employee turnover is likely to have an effect on you. Consider the following scenarios for "X Company."

You've been a **customer** for years and like the prices and convenience. Even though the new employees are nice, you don't like their lack of knowledge about the products, prices, promotions, placement, programs, policies, and procedures. You especially don't like the fact that they don't know you and your preferences. You really don't like to change, but you're thinking of taking your business elsewhere.

You're an **employee** and you like your co-workers. However, you don't like the fact that your supervisor is more concerned about you being late occasionally than how hard you work when you're there. You're thinking of looking for another job where your efforts are appreciated.

You're a **supervisor** and you like the responsibility. However, you don't like constantly having to replace your best employees, though you can't blame them for leaving for more money. You spend most of your time interviewing and training new recruits or issuing warnings to your staff. You find it hard to motivate employees who don't seem to care, and management is less gratifying than you thought it would be.

2 "Turnover and What to Do about It," *Cornell Hotel & Restaurant Administration Quarterly* (February 1, 1992).

You're the **trainer** and you like sharing your knowledge, but you don't like constantly training new recruits who don't stay with the company very long. You're beginning to ask yourself if your efforts really make a difference.

You're working in **human resources** and you like utilizing your people skills. At times, you feel overwhelmed with termination and new-hire paperwork. You don't have as much time as you'd like to resolve employee issues. You're beginning to wonder if you made the right career choice.

You're the **financial officer** and you like keeping the ship afloat. However, you don't like having to reduce staff levels to offset declining sales. This is a difficult decision to make, but if sales keep declining, you won't have much choice.

You're a **stockholder** and have held shares in the company for years. Even though the recent layoffs have had a positive impact on the stock price, you don't like the declining sales. You're beginning to question management's ability and whether owning the stock is a good long-term investment.

High employee turnover rates clearly have negative effects; that's why companies continually search for ways to reduce employee turnover. They provide their supervisors with training on the best recruiting, interviewing, hiring, reviewing, and coaching practices. They incorporate employee turnover goals in bonus programs and Management by Objective programs (MBO). When these goals are not achieved, managers sometimes rationalize that not all turnover is bad. Some companies have begun to view turnover as just part of doing business, while others are spending millions of dollars in consulting fees to reduce turnover.

The 5-Step Performance Compensation Program reduces employee turnover and benefits everyone involved with the company—whether you're a customer, employee, supervisor, trainer, human resources specialist, financial officer, or stockholder. As you will see in the next chapter, the 5-Step Performance Compensation Program also helps companies achieve the six goals common to every business.

Chapter 2

The 6 Goals of Every Business

All companies share the six goals listed below regardless of their size or industry, and meeting these goals is critical to their success. We will examine the importance of each, how they're all interlinked, and how the 5-Step Performance Compensation Program helps companies achieve these goals.

The 6 Goals of Every Business
1. Increase profits.
2. Reduce staffing requirements.
3. Increase productivity.
4. Have the best employees.
5. Increase employee performance.
6. Motivate employees to try their best.

Profitability—The Bottom Line

Profits are the number one goal of every company. They're the lifeblood of an organization; they allow it to thrive and survive. Profits provide the resources necessary to maintain and expand ongoing operations. Programs designed to increase profits focus on either increasing revenue or reducing costs. The 5-Step Performance Compensation Program offers the benefits of both.

- **Reduce costs.** The 5-Step Performance Compensation Program reduces turnover costs by retaining your best employees. Retaining high-productivity employees will reduce your overall staff requirements. Retaining experienced employees will reduce costly errors.
- **Increase revenue.** The 5-Step Performance Compensation Program increases sales by retaining experienced employees who are more knowledgeable about your products and services. Knowledgeable employees are able to offer your customers the best solutions to satisfy their needs.

Wall Street and its investors will rally behind any cost-reduction move a company makes. Investors aren't concerned with how cost reductions are implemented; they only see them as numbers on an income statement that improve the bottom line. Any payroll cost-reduction plan can also have an immediate positive impact on profits. Only a well-conceived cost-reduction plan like the 5-Step Performance Compensation Program can provide positive, long-term results that will satisfy the needs of Wall Street and Main Street.

Staffing—The Human Resource

From my experience, having the right people at the right place and at the right time is essential to maximize labor productivity. Staffing models vary by industry and are used as a "rule of thumb" to measure employee productivity. Proper staffing levels reduce both wasteful overtime and idle time. The following are some simple staffing examples:

Example 1: Call Center staffing requirements are based upon calls received per day. This model is calculated using calls received per day, average calls answered per agent, and average absenteeism. Example: 1,000 calls divided by 40 calls answered per day, equals 25 agents. Adding 10 percent for absenteeism equals 28 agents.

Example 2: Retail staffing requirements are based upon sales or 8 percent as a rule of thumb. This model is calculated using sales per day and average wages per associate. Example: $3,000 in sales per day times 8 percent model equals $240. Multiply the $10 average wage times 8 hours per day, and it equals $80. Divide $240 by $80, and it equals 3 associates.

Example 3: Warehouse staffing requirements are based on orders per day. This model is calculated using orders received per day, average orders pulled per worker, and average absenteeism. Example: 1,000 orders per day divided by 70 orders pulled per day equals 14 workers. Adding 10 percent for absenteeism equals 16 workers.

The variables in workflow on an hourly, daily, weekly, monthly, seasonal, or cyclical basis make staffing much more complicated than illustrated here. These simple examples are designed to show how averages play a major role in calculating proper staff requirements. The fewest number of employees with the highest productivity is the ideal model, such as the one offered in the 5-Step Performance Compensation Program.

Productivity—The Payoff

Productivity measures employee output and efficiency. It can be calculated as revenue per employee, labor cost as a percentage of sales, or profit per employee. No matter how you measure it, higher productivity equals higher profitability. Companies continuously look for ways to increase productivity to stay competitive.

For example, technology investment in recent years has paid off with big productivity gains. Sales analysis helps distributors and retailers determine which products are the most profitable. Inventory management systems help manufacturers, distributors, and retailers keep inventories at optimum levels to reduce warehouse expenses and finance charges. Historical data along with sales forecasts help determine proper scheduling. Scheduling programs are used to determine optimum staffing levels. Productivity analysis shows your best employees have the lowest cost per unit produced. Every department has employees with productivity that far exceeds the group average. Managers will say they wouldn't need as many employees if all of them were like their top performers.

Our global economy requires companies to react quickly to changes in the marketplace. High productivity allows companies to adapt to our rapidly changing environment. Employee output is the backbone of a company's productivity. A strong backbone gives a company the ability to remain competitive and profitable. For this reason, companies need new employees to come up to speed as soon as possible. The 5-Step Performance Compensation Program encourages rapid employee development by empowering supervisors to engage them with recognition for above-average performance.

Hire the Best—Retain Your Best Employees

Hiring new employees is a gamble that deserves careful consideration. It's a decision you'll have to live with—like renting a room in your home to a stranger. Managers use the best practices in recruiting, interviewing, and screening to aid them with their hiring decisions, and these activities cost time and money.

- Companies spend time and money *recruiting* applicants. Costs vary depending on the type of advertising used on Web postings, newspaper ads, or job fairs.
- Companies spend time and money *interviewing* applicants. Managers spend up to one to two hours scheduling and conducting an interview. It takes two or three interviews to find a qualified applicant.
- Companies spend time and money *screening* applicants with background, credit, and drug checks. These costs vary depending on the type and number of screening checks required.

Recruiting, interviewing, hiring, and training new employees requires a great deal of hard work. Training departments spend the majority of their resources on new-hire training, yet positive results are not guaranteed because new employee performance and retention is uncertain. Individuals assigned to these tasks can become disillusioned when high turnover makes it seem like a revolving door of new employees. If a company's balance sheet listed labor as an asset, the value would be based upon productivity. Above-average employees would be considered high-value assets and companies would include them in their asset loss prevention programs. Without a retention program, these activities are reduced to merely busy work. The one thing many companies are missing is a program like the 5-Step Performance Compensation Program to break the endless turnover cycle.

Performance—The Measurement

People like to know how they're performing at all times. This is one of the reasons golf is such a popular sport. The average or expected number of strokes for each golf hole is posted as "par." This is where the expression "par for the course" comes from. Golf defines performance with the double-bogey, bogey, par, birdie, and eagle. Golfers know how they're doing after every hole, and they know that every shot counts. With practice and dedication, golfers can achieve a scratch handicap or average performance. The same is true in business.

Employees like to know how they're doing on the job at all times. New employees must learn the basics and what I refer to as the "Ps" of a business. These are the products, prices, promotions, programs, people, policies, and procedures. The learning curve for these basic skills will vary depending upon the employee's prior experience, knowledge, and the number of products and services offered. Management expects new employees to achieve average performance within the ninety-day review period. These performance expectations increase with the amount of time in the position. The following are the different across-the-board performance levels I've experienced with the entry-level employees I've hired.

> **Double Bogey:** New golfers get more excited with a good shot than they do with a bad shot because they're still learning the basic techniques and their expectations are lower. In a "double bogey" hiring situation, *all* new-employee performance is unsatisfactory within the first

ninety days of employment as the new employees learn the basic business skills.

Bogey: New golfers strive to meet the average or "par" as they practice the basic techniques. In a "bogey" hiring situation, *most* new-employee performance is below average within the first ninety days of employment while they practice the basic business skills.

Par: Golfers continue to practice their skills and strive to exceed the average or "under par." In a "par" hiring situation, about 40 percent of new-employee performance is considered "good" or "competent" within the first ninety days of employment.

Birdie: Experienced golfers don't get as excited with a good shot as they get upset with a bad shot because their expectations are higher. In a "birdie" hiring situation, about 20 percent of new-employee performance is above average within the first ninety days of employment.

Eagle: All golfers dream of getting an eagle or hole-in-one, which is a rare event even with years of practice. In an "eagle" hiring situation, about 10 percent of new-employee performance is outstanding within the first ninety days of employment.

Supervisors often wish their employees would try their best every day, and they want to get them up to speed as soon as possible. They hope their employees will achieve above-average performance, and they pray that their best employees won't leave the company for better opportunities. Unfortunately, wishing, wanting, hoping, and praying are not the best formulas for success.

Companies usually roll out the red carpet for new employees during the recruiting, interviewing, hiring, and training processes. Soon after basic training is over, they are often given less attention until their ninety-day probationary review. A sink or swim training approach is sometimes used to motivate new employees to become self-sufficient. This is a risky strategy because they already feel like fish out of water due to their lack of basic knowledge. If we treated new customers in this same fashion, we would risk losing them to our competition; the same is true for new employees. The 5-Step Performance Compensation Program keeps management and employees focused on performance during every stage of their development.

Motivation—What's Important

Supervisors have two primary tools they use to motivate their employees—raises and corrective action, which are sometimes referred to as "the carrot and the stick." Both are powerful tools that influence employee performance.

- **Raises** let employees know they're doing a good job and the company appreciates their efforts. Managers can reward employee performance after the probationary period and the annual review.
- **Corrective action** lets employees know what they're doing wrong and shows them how to become good corporate citizens. Corrective action can be issued at any time for a number of reasons, which is why it's the most commonly used management tool.

Following one of my presentations, I met Sarah from the Employers Group, who was a professional and seasoned manager of unemployment insurance services. She asked me to call her as soon as my book was published so she could give the owner of her company a copy. She said he agreed with my philosophy about motivating employees and was in the process of revamping their company's entire pay structure. Her company represented employers in contested unemployment hearings and stressed the need for proper documentation in defending such cases. She explained how companies pay unemployment reserves based upon the number of claims made against them. She told us of changes in California unemployment laws that were intended to reduce turnover. One regional manager in the audience commented, "We won't have all these issues after we start Mark's program." Then our human resources manager added, "We have very few employee issues in Mark's customer service department." The 5-Step Performance Compensation Program emphasizes positive feedback to motivate and retain employees.

Considering the six goals every company has, here are the questions that need to be answered:

- What can you do to motivate employees to try their best?
- What can you do to increase employee performance?
- What can you do to have the best employees?
- What can you do to increase productivity?
- What can you do to reduce staffing requirements?
- What can you do to increase profits?

Each of those questions has the same answer: implement the 5-Step Performance Compensation Program explained in the next chapter.

Chapter 3

The 5-Step Performance Compensation Program

The 5-Step Performance Compensation Program matches the employee pay level with his or her performance level. This is the best way to retain your best employees and ensure you're not paying for more than what you're getting out of your employees. It's a simple 5-step process:

Step 1: Start entry-level positions below the industry's average pay levels.
Step 2: Clearly define performance goals.
Step 3: Post employee performance results daily.
Step 4: Give employees performance feedback on a regular basis.
Step 5: Give pay adjustments for above-average performance on a periodic basis.

How It Works—5 Simple Steps

Step 1: Start entry-level positions below the industry's average pay levels.
New employee performance varies dramatically during the first ninety days. You don't know how a new recruit will perform until after they start working, and trainee performance is always below average.

Check Web sites like salary.com to make sure your *average* wage level is competitive for your area. Be sure to include your recognition and reward system as part of your recruiting, interviewing, hiring, training, and review processes. Explaining advancement programs during recruitment will attract ambitious employees, discussing expectations during an interview will help eliminate applicants who are not willing to work hard and prove their ability, and setting expectations during training will help employees know where to concentrate their efforts.

Step 2: Clearly define performance goals.
When defining goals, use group performance averages because they're easily understood and accepted by employees.

Step 3: Post employee performance results daily.
It's important to post performance results daily because employees try harder when their performance is publicly displayed.

Step 4: Give performance feedback on a regular basis.
Periodic performance reviews will reinforce the priorities set by management, and coaching during performance reviews helps keep employees focused on where they need to improve.

Step 5: Give pay adjustments for above-average performance on a periodic basis.
Employees try to do their best every day when they know their pay level is related to their performance level. Raises should be determined by the same percentage or amount (e.g., 2 to 4 percent, or $.25 to $.50 per hour). It won't motivate your employees if you nickel and dime them. Pay grade promotions can be as much as $1.00 per hour. Match pay levels with performance levels as quickly as possible.

Tools for Implementing Performance-Based Compensation

Wage Models
The following are two examples of wage models that can be used to make sure an employee's pay level matches his or her performance level.

Performance Model Example

- **Training** or 40% below average performance = 20% below the industry's average wages
- **Learning** or 20% below average performance = 10% below the industry's average wages
- **Competent** or average performance = the industry's average wages
- **Exceeds** or 20% above average performance = 10% above the industry's average wages
- **Outstanding** or 40% above average performance = 20% above the industry's average wages

Scenario: Sue, Jane, and Kim are all in training. Sue is 20 percent below average in productivity, Jane is average in productivity, and Kim is 20 percent above average in productivity.

Jane and Kim met or exceeded performance expectations in a short time and merit pay adjustments. Sue was still learning the basics and we want to continue to monitor her progress. The goal is to match employee compensation to performance to ensure employees are neither underpaid nor overpaid. Employees need to know their compensation level is based upon their performance level, and pay increases are only issued when performance increases.

Pay-Grade Level Model Example

- **Level I** or Apprentice = $8 to $10 per hour
- **Level II** or Graduate = $9 to $11 per hour
- **Level III** or Top Performer = $10 to $12 per hour
- **Level IV** or Leads = $11 to $13 per hour

Implementation Models
Here are three different methods to implement the 5-Step Performance Compensation Program based upon the size of your business.

Model 1—Monthly Performance Review (for small organizations)
This method is appropriate for smaller and less formal businesses. All it takes is a monthly review of performance and then making pay adjustments in relationship to the averages.

- Establish performance and pay level guidelines using industry averages wages in your area.
- Performance expectations should be adjusted for time in position. For example, if a new employee has "average" performance within their first three months, that would be considered "above expectations."
- Reward employees who meet or beat performance expectations and continue until the pay level matches employee performance levels. Monthly rewards for above-average performance and below-average earners will keep employees focused on what's important.

Model 2—Quarterly Review Program (for larger organizations)
Formal, written performance reviews are more appropriate for larger and more formal organizations. Meet with employees on a monthly basis to review their performance and quarterly pay increase potential.

- New employees must have average quality, productivity, and attendance and be in good standing with the company at their **ninety-day (or three-month)** probationary review. Reward new employees who have *met* performance standards with pay increases as much as $1.00 per hour.
- Employees with **six months** of experience must have above-average quality, productivity, and attendance and be in good standing with the company. Reward those employees who have *exceeded* your performance standards in this short time with pay increases as much as $1.00 per hour.

- Employees with **nine months** of experience must have above-average quality, productivity, and attendance and be in good standing with the company. Reward those employees who have continued to exceed your performance standards with pay increases as much as $1.00 per hour.

- Employees with **twelve months** of experience must have above-average quality, productivity, and attendance and be in good standing with the company. Reward those employees who have continued to exceed your performance standards with pay increases as much as $1.00 per hour. Continue this process until the pay level reaches the maximum or ceiling for the job function.

Model 3—Pay Grade System (for large organizations)

Establish skill and performance level guidelines with pay grades or ranges. Time in position may or may not be required for advancement. Employees may be certified ahead of time for future positions like lead, supervisor, assistant manager, and manager. This will enable the company to move quickly when openings become available and reduce transition times. Employee retention will increase when an employee's career path is predetermined within the company.

- **Level I** or **Apprentice** probationary review requires average performance, good attendance, and good standing with the company. The employee must maintain a passing grade on all job function skill tests. Reward those new employees who have met performance standards with pay increases of as much as $.50.

- **Level II** or **Graduate** requires a minimum of six months of experience and consistent 20 percent above-average performance. The employee must maintain a passing grade on all job function skill tests, must have good attendance, and must be in good standing with the company.

- **Level III** or **Top Performer** requires a minimum of nine months of experience and consistent 30 percent above-average performance. The employee must maintain a passing grade on all job function skill tests, must have good attendance, and must be in good standing with the company.

- **Level IV** or **Lead** requires a minimum of twelve months of experience and consistent 40 percent above-average performance. The employee maintain a passing grade on all job function skill tests, must have good attendance, and must be in good standing with the company.

Note: These programs must be administered fairly to be effective. Employees must know this is a performance contest, not a popularity contest.

Myths about Performance Compensation Programs

There are a couple of myths about Performance Compensation Programs: The first is that Performance Compensation Programs award too many raises. The reality is, while employees may consider all pay increases as raises, most are merely pay adjustments to match an employee's performance. Pay increases are only considered raises after an employee reaches the industry average wage level.

The second myth is that Performance Compensation Programs award pay increases too quickly and easily. In reality, pay adjustments are only awarded when performance standards are met within the first ninety days in position or exceeded after the probationary period ends. The frequency of these pay adjustments should be limited only by the pace of the employee's performance.

Now that you understand *how* the 5-Step Performance Compensation Program works, it's time to look at *why* it works—why it's so effective at reducing both bottom-line costs and employee turnover.

Chapter 4

Why Pay More?

The 5-Step Performance Compensation Program decreases bottom-line costs while increasing productivity. Below are two payroll cost examples; the first is the cost of payroll for a company that has not implemented a Performance Compensation Program, the second is the cost for that same company after implementing a Performance Compensation Program.

Payroll Cost Scenario without a Performance Compensation Program

You have five employees and no Performance Compensation Program. You have one employee at each of the five performance levels. You pay all employees the industry average wage of $12.00 with a budgeted hourly cost of **$60.00.** You're not satisfied with the two employees who are below average in performance, and you may lose the two employees who are above average in performance because they aren't happy with their compensation. Without a Performance Compensation Program, you end up replacing non-average employees until all you have is average performance.

Payroll Cost Scenario with a Performance Compensation Program

You have five employees and have implemented a Performance Compensation Program. You have one employee at each of the five performance levels. You would pay each employee based upon his or her performance level, (i.e. $9.60, $10.80, $12.00, $13.20, and $14.40 per hour). The average wage is $12.00 with an hourly cost of **$60.00.** You and your employees are happy because their pay level matches their performance level.

Employees with a Performance Compensation Program are motivated to increase their performance. When all your employees are 20 percent above average in performance, you would only need a staff of four. You would pay each 10 percent above industry average wages, or $13.20 per hour, with an hourly cost of only **$52.80**. You and your employees are happy because their pay and performance levels are above average. Your finance department is happy because you're under budget. Your human resources department is happy because you have low employee turnover.

Company owners keep a close watch on the bottom line. Reducing costs is one of their primary goals. Much of their attention is directed at payroll costs because it is often the single largest business expense. The conventional labor model focuses on low wages as a way to reduce payroll costs. The 5-Step Performance Compensation Program takes the opposite approach to achieve this goal and with better results. I created the following illustrations to show how you can pay your way to prosperity. When I showed them to the Maly's CFO, he quickly commented, "A picture tells a thousand words."

The Cost Benefit Illustrated

Illustration #1 shows staff requirements and payroll costs for various performance levels:

Performance	Average orders per month	Average orders per day	Data entry per hour	Required hours per day	Add 10% absenteeism	FTE required	Hourly wages	$ per order	Annual Payroll
Unsatisfactory -40%	68000	3400	3	1133	1247	166	$9.60	$3.20	$3,319,125
Below average -20%	68000	3400	4	850	935	125	$10.80	$2.70	$2,800,512
Average	68000	3400	5	680	748	100	$12.00	$2.40	$2,489,344
Above average +20%	68000	3400	6	567	623	83	$13.20	$2.20	$2,281,899
Outstanding +40%	68000	3400	7	486	534	71	$14.40	$2.06	$2,133,723

This illustration shows how staff requirements decrease as productivity levels increase. Wage increases are offset by these lower staff requirements. In other words, it takes an army of new and inexperienced employees to do what a small team of well-trained and motivated employees can do at a lower cost. Below are formulas for this table:

If every employee has **unsatisfactory** performance:

> Below-average orders per hour -40% = 3
> Number of hours needed per day 3,400 / 3 = 1133
> Add absenteeism 1133 x 1.1 = 1247 hours
> Number of F/T employees needed is 1247 / 7.5 = 166
> Unsatisfactory average wage -20% = $9.60
> Cost per order $9.60 / 3 = $3.20
> Annual cost is $9.60 x 166 agents x 2080 hours = **$3,319,125**

If every employee has **below-average** performance:

> Below-average orders per hour -20% = 4
> Number of hours needed per day 3,400 / 4 = 850

Add absenteeism 850 x 1.1 = 935 scheduled hours
Number of F/T employees needed is 935 / 7.5 = 125
Below-average wage -10% = $10.80 per hour
Cost per order $10.80 / 4 = $2.70
Annual cost is $10.80 x 125 agents x 2080 hours = **$2,800,512**

If every employee has **average** performance:

Average orders per hour = 5
Number of hours needed per day 3,400 / 5 = 680
Add absenteeism 680 x 1.1 = 748 scheduled hours
Number of F/T employees needed is 748 / 7.5 = 100
Average wage = $12.00 per hour
Cost per order $12.00 / 5 = $2.40
Annual cost is $12.00 x 100 agents x 2080 hours = **$2,489,344**

If every employee has **above-average** performance:

Above-average orders per hour +20% = 6
Number of hours needed per day 3,400 / 6 = 567
Add absenteeism 567 x 1.1 = 623 scheduled hours
Number of F/T employees needed is 623 / 7.5 = 83
Above-average wage 10% = $13.20 per hour
Cost per order $13.20 / 6 = $2.20
Annual cost is $13.20 x 83 agents x 2080 hours = **$2,281,899**

If every employee has **outstanding** performance:

Above-average orders per hour +40% = 7
Number of hours needed per day 3,400 / 7 = 486
Add absenteeism 486 x 1.1 = 534 scheduled hours
Number of F/T employees needed is 534 / 7.5 = 71
Above-average wage +20% = $14.40 per hour
Cost per order $14.40 / 7 = $2.06
Annual cost is $14.40 x 71 agents x 2080 hours = **$2,133,723**

Companies that try to keep payroll costs down by keeping wages low have higher turnover rates. It's like always taking the lowest bid for all purchases. The lowest bid isn't always the best value because these products usually don't have the same quality and have to be replaced more often. The same is true for new employees who are a gamble since they don't have a proven performance record. New employees are less productive and usually don't stay with the company as long as experienced employees with good performance records.

The Bottom Line

- Average wages are increased 10 percent per hour if every employee is 20 percent above average in productivity.
- Staff requirements are reduced 17 percent if every employee is 20 percent above average in productivity.
- Payroll costs are reduced 8 percent if every employee is 20 percent above average in productivity.

Managing is easier when you spend your time catching employees doing a good job. It's fun to give recognition, rewards, awards, and incentives. It may be hard to understand the motivational impact a $.50 raise has on an employee's performance, but I've witnessed the tears of joy when employee performance is recognized and rewarded. Motivated employees require less coaching and counseling, as well as fewer warnings and performance agreements. Employees under the 5-Step Performance Compensation Program know what's important and manage themselves.

Constant turnover of your best employees places a strain on your organization. Consider these two unlikely hypothetical events: Would you notice if the bottom 10 percent of your staff won the lottery and left the company tomorrow? Would you notice if the top 10 percent of your staff won the lottery and left the company tomorrow?

Illustration #2 shows the annual payroll cost for two employees who were hired on January 1st. The first started at industry average wages, and the second started at below industry average wages with a quarterly performance compensation program:

Hourly	Jan-06	Feb-06	Mar-06	Apr-06	May-06	Jun-06	Jul-06	Aug-06	Sep-06	Oct-06	Nov-06	Dec-06	Annual
$14.00													
$13.50													
$13.00										$2,249	$2,249	$2,249	**$23,874**
$12.50													
$12.00	$2,076	$2,076	$2,076	$2,076	$2,076	$2,076	$2,076	$2,076	$2,076	$2,076	$2,076	$2,076	$24,912
$11.50													
$11.00				$1,903	$1,903	$1,903							
$10.50													
$10.00	$1,730	$1,730	$1,730										
Savings													$1,038

The *first* employee was hired at the industry average wage of $12 per hour and hasn't received any raises, resulting in an annual cost of $24,912. There is no relationship between their pay and their performance. They may not have proven their capabilities because there is no incentive to do so. If they've exceeded expectations, they may feel their efforts aren't appreciated and may not be motivated to seek more responsibility; they may be looking for better opportunities outside your department or company.

The *second* employee was hired at $10 per hour and received three $1.00 quarterly performance raises in a row, resulting in an annual cost of $23,874. They have been trained on what's important and their pay is tied to their performance. Exceeding department standards gives them a sense of accomplishment, and they feel their efforts are appreciated. They're motivated and looking for more responsibility and opportunity within your organization.

The annual payroll savings in this example is $1,038. While hiring at industry average wage levels may help in recruiting new employees, it doesn't guarantee good results. New employee productivity is always below average and their pay should reflect their training performance. Start new employees 20 percent below industry average wage and offer an aggressive performance reward system.

Illustration #3 shows the annual payroll costs for two employees who were both hired on January 1st. The first started at industry average wages, and the second started at below industry average wages with a monthly performance compensation program:

Hourly	Jan-06	Feb-06	Mar-06	Apr-06	May-06	Jun-06	Jul-06	Aug-06	Sep-06	Oct-06	Nov-06	Dec-06	Annual
$14.00													
$13.50													
$13.00							$2,249	$2,249	$2,249	$2,249	$2,249	$2,249	$25,172
$12.50						$2,163							
$12.00	$2,076	$2,076	$2,076	$2,076	$2,076	$2,076	$2,076	$2,076	$2,076	$2,076	$2,076	$2,076	$24,912
$11.50				$1,990									
$11.00			$1,903										
$10.50		$1,817											
$10.00	$1,730												
Cost													$ (260)

The *first* employee was hired at the industry average wage of $12 per hour and hasn't received any raises, resulting in an annual cost of $24,912. There is no relationship between their pay and their performance. They may not have proven their capabilities because there is no incentive to do so. If they've exceeded expectations, they may feel their efforts aren't appreciated and may not be motivated to seek more responsibility; they may be looking for better opportunities outside your department or company.

The *second* employee was hired at $10 per hour and received six $.50 performance raises in a row, resulting in an annual cost of $25,172. They have been trained on what's important and their pay is tied to their performance. Exceeding department standards gives them a sense of accomplishment, and they feel their efforts are appreciated. They're motivated and looking for more responsibility and opportunity within your organization.

Which of these employees would you want to have on your team? Is having a well-trained and motivated employee worth the additional $260 cost? A Performance Compensation Program provides the employee with a roadmap for success and trains them on what's important by rewarding their achievements. This small cost difference is offset by higher productivity gains.

The Rewards of a Performance Compensation Program

It's human nature to constantly want more, and we forget to appreciate what we already have. Employees think it's easy to find another job that will pay more money. They forget that though the grass may be greener on the other side, it's still a job where they have to work (or mow). Managers rationalize that everyone can be replaced when an employee leaves the company for more money. They forget how much time and money it takes to find a good employee. A Performance Compensation Program reminds managers to reward their best employees. Rewards help remind employees how fortunate they are to work for a company that appreciates their hard work.

- **R**ecognize and reward employee performance.
- **E**mployees don't leave for better opportunities.
- **W**age increases for above-average performance increases productivity.
- **A**ll-star productivity reduces staff requirements.
- **R**educe payroll costs with lower staff levels.
- **D**ecreased payroll costs improve the bottom line.

The Millennium Generation has been trained since grade school to expect recognition and rewards for their accomplishments. Businesses haven't found a way to meet these expectations. The standard model tries to keep payroll costs down by focusing on keeping wages low. Low wages encourage above-average performers to leave the company for better opportunities. This constant turnover keeps productivity at low levels. Low productivity increases staff requirements and ends up increasing your overall payroll costs. The 5-Step Performance Compensation Program takes the opposite approach by increasing both wages and productivity to lower staff requirements.

Who Else Uses Performance Compensation Programs?

For twelve years, I've been using the 5-Step Performance Compensation Program and promoting its benefits to my colleagues. I've been asked what other companies use this to motivate and retain their employees.

I found the first example during a visit with a lifelong friend and successful hair salon owner. We had gone to school and worked together. I was in his wedding and rented a room from him and his wife before the birth of their first daughter. It had been a year since our last get-together and he asked, "What's new?" I told him I was writing a book about reducing employee turnover. As a small business owner, he understood how time-consuming turnover could be because he was the trainer. He admitted it had taken several years to "get it through his thick head" that you get more from your employees when you pay more. His retail sales quadrupled and profits doubled when he increased commissions. He said my program sounded like one his daughter experienced at Cingular where she had started in customer service at $10 per hour and then received several performance increases over three years. She liked working there so much that she turned down an offer for more money from another company. My friend was very proud of his daughter's achievements. I was excited to finally find an example of a large and well-known company that used a Performance Compensation Program to motivate and retain their employees.

I found the second example during one of my Performance Compensation Presentations. A Maly's Store regional manager said this program sounded similar to one where her older sister worked. Since 1989, RxAmerica, owned by Longs Drug Stores, had been a leading benefits manager with a national retail network of 55,000 pharmacies. Her sister started at $10 per hour and received several quarterly performance increases over two years. She liked working there so much that it was the first job her sister had ever stayed with for more than a few months.

The third example came from my customer service trainer, who told me about a similar program where her friend's son worked. Since 1991, Interstate Batteries had been number one in marketing and distribution with a national network of 300 distributors and 200,000 retail dealers. They used a quarterly performance review program, and her friend's son liked working there so much, he rehired even after being laid-off during a slow period in the industry.

There's a reason why employees like working for companies that use a Performance Compensation Program—the pay matches the employees' performance. Their efforts and accomplishments are recognized and rewarded. In the next chapter, you will see how happy employees create a chain reaction that positively affects the entire company.

Chapter 5

The Impact

Owners and executives carefully consider the impact any program will have on their organization before implementing it. Companies are only as good as their weakest link. These weak links cause a chain reaction and have negative effects on an organization.

The Chain Reaction Illustrated

Chain Reaction without a Performance Compensation Program

- No recognition and reward = unmotivated employees
- Unmotivated employees = below-average performance
- Below-average performance = below-average wages
- Below-average wages = higher turnover
- Higher turnover = lower experience levels
- Lower experience levels = lower productivity and **more errors**
- Lower productivity = higher staff requirements
- Higher staff requirements = higher payroll cost
- Higher payroll cost = lower profits
- **More errors** = less customer satisfaction
- Less customer satisfaction = more opportunity for your competition
- More opportunity for your competition = less sales for you

Policies designed to accomplish one goal may have unintended effects. Standard review and reward policies are designed to keep payroll costs down by keeping hourly wages down. The effect is low employee motivation, causing higher turnover and reduced productivity. Low productivity increases staffing requirements, causing higher payroll costs. Changing your review and reward policies can break this cycle. Standard review practices limit management's ability to motivate employees. Performance Compensation Programs remove these restraints and create a positive chain reaction in your organization that will look like the following.

Chain Reaction with a Performance Compensation Program

- Recognition and reward = motivated employees
- Motivated employees = above-average performance
- Above-average performance = above-average wages
- Above-average wages = lower turnover
- Lower turnover = higher experience levels
- Higher experience levels = higher productivity with **fewer errors**
- Higher productivity = lower staff requirements
- Lower staff requirements = less payroll cost
- Less payroll cost = higher profits
- **Fewer errors** = more customer satisfaction
- More customer satisfaction = less opportunity for your competition
- Less opportunity for your competition = more sales for you

Once you start this positive chain reaction, you'll never want to go back to the old way of managing employees.

Benefits of the 5-Step Performance Compensation Program

Standard reviews are given at the end of the probation period and at the end of the year. Raises are limited to a budgeted cost-of-living increase. Employees need to see some systematic form of advancement or they end up leaving the company. They will often accept lower pay positions for the possibility of improving their career. Companies that aren't satisfied with high turnover and low productivity are ready for something different. You can't expect different results if you keep using a system that's not working. Performance Compensation Programs reduce turnover, increase productivity, lower staffing requirements, and improve the bottom line.

Benefits include:

- Fewer employees
- Less payroll
- Lower payroll taxes
- Lower benefit costs
- Less equipment
- Less space
- Lower turnover
- Fewer recruiting costs
- Fewer interviewing costs
- Fewer applicant screening costs
- Less paperwork for human resources
- Fewer training costs
- Fewer errors
- Less shrinkage
- More sales

How Employee Retention Affects Everyone Involved

Earlier, we looked at how employee turnover negatively affects everyone involved with a company. Now let's take a look at how the opposite scenario—employee retention—positively affects those same people.

As a **customer,** you like how helpful and friendly the employees are. They know the products, prices, promotions, placement, programs, policies, and procedures. You especially like the fact that they know you and really seem to care. You can't think of any reason why you would do business elsewhere.

As an **employee,** you feel your efforts are really appreciated. Your supervisor is always trying to catch you doing a good job and cares more about your performance than your being late once in a while. You try your best every day and are looking for more responsibility and opportunities within the company.

As a **supervisor,** you like how hard your employees work. You like spending time reviewing performance results, coaching, and rewarding above-average performers. Your employees seem to manage themselves and you rarely have to issue warnings. You find management gratifying and rewarding.

As a **trainer,** you like teaching new employees the business basics. Trainees get excited and pay close attention after you explain the 5-Step Performance Compensation Program. You're proud when your trainees succeed and you know your efforts will have a big impact on the company for years.

As a **human resources specialist,** you like the low employee turnover and having less paperwork because of it. You have plenty of time to utilize your people skills to resolve the occasional employee issues. You feel like you really make a difference in your work.

As a **financial officer,** you like the increasing sales and the productivity of your employees. You have no problem getting additional financing for your growing operation. The bottom-line profits on the financial statement make you look good, and you're proud to work for a company that has so much potential.

As a **stockholder,** you like how the stock consistently performs well. The company continues to grow along with sales. You have confidence in management's ability and plan to hold the stock as a long-term investment.

It's hard to believe that one simple program can satisfy everyone's needs the way this one does. For over twelve years, I have personally witnessed these benefits using the 5-Step Performance Compensation Program with 900 entry-level employees at two companies in two different industries.

Chapter 6

Questions & Answers

Q: *What's the catch?*

A: The 5-Step Performance Compensation Program doesn't guarantee all employees will be successful. The fact is, 10 percent of new employees will achieve superstar success, and 10 percent will fail with or without any program. A Performance Compensation Program focuses on managing the 80 percent who fall between these two extremes. It motivates the majority of your employees to do above-average work month after month, and it trains them to try their best consistently. It may take some employees longer to meet your performance standards, but they keep on trying. You'll be willing to give marginal performers additional time to meet your standards when their starting hourly wage is below the industry average.

Q: *Doesn't increasing wages to lower payroll costs seem counterintuitive?*

A: Yes, it does seem counterintuitive. However, Performance Compensation Programs lower payroll costs by raising productivity and lowering staff requirements.

Q: *Doesn't giving several raises sound like crazy talk?*

A: Yes, at first glance it does. However, talking about spending so much time and money recruiting, hiring, and training employees—only to lose them to our competition—is the true crazy talk.

Q: *Doesn't a Performance Compensation Program defy conventional wisdom?*

A: Yes, it is an unconventional program. The question is, where's the wisdom of using conventional practices if they're not working? After all, isn't doing the same thing and expecting different results the definition of insanity?

Q: *Can Performance Compensation Programs work in other departments?*

A: The 5-Step Performance Compensation Program is designed for any entry-level positions.

Q: *I thought money wasn't a motivator.*

A: Most people have heard of this from Maslow's hierarchy of needs model. They forget this principle applies to higher wage levels where money becomes less important. Money is a huge motivator for entry-level positions.

Q: *Don't studies show the number one reason employees leave their job is due to their supervisor?*

A: Yes, they do. When you look at the underlying reasons, you'll find two things: the employee felt the supervisor didn't appreciate how hard he or she worked and only noticed when the employee did something wrong. A Performance Compensation Program provides supervisors the tools to turn this situation around.

Q: *How does the 5-Step Performance Compensation Program motivate a tenure employee who doesn't seem to care or try anymore?*

A: If an employee doesn't want to play, it's their choice. However, the 5-Step Performance Compensation Program pays only those who do. Usually, employees who see their co-workers getting recognition and rewards want to get back in the game.

Q: *What if an employee stops trying or performing after receiving a raise?*

A: Performance Compensation Programs works both ways. Above-average wage earners are expected to maintain above-average performance levels. Don't hesitate to give performance reviews or take corrective action when necessary.

Q: *What if employees work together to lower the average productivity?*

A: Employees organize when they don't feel they're treated fairly or rewarded for their performance. A Performance Compensation Program encourages individual performance.

Q: *Do average performance levels increase as employees work harder?*

A: Not really. Your best employees end up getting promoted or transferred inside and outside of a company and move up the corporate ladder. They're replaced with new trainees with below-average performance. My experience has found that average productivity doesn't change; only the people change. Your goal is to retain above-average performers for a longer period.

Q: *Doesn't giving raises too quickly set a bad precedent?*

A: A Performance Compensation Program is targeted at entry-level positions and wages. Skilled professionals are hired at the normal or above-average industry wages and expect the conventional performance review schedule.

Q: *Doesn't the 5-Step Performance Compensation Program sound like a bleeding heart program for employees?*

A: At first glance, it does. However, the 5-Step Performance Compensation Program was created to reduce turnover, which has been bleeding companies dry for years.

Q: *What is the recommended amount of these pay adjustments?*

A: This can vary by department, company, or industry. I recommend all raises be the same percentage or amount, such as 2 to 4 percent or $.25 to $.50 per hour. Pay grade promotions can be as much as $1.00 per hour. Raises must be earned and meaningful for the employee. It doesn't motivate employees when you nickel and dime them. The goal is to match pay levels with performance levels as soon as possible.

Q: *How can I get management to approve the 5-Step Performance Compensation Program?*

A: All companies seek higher productivity from their employees. Above-average employees are more productive than below-average employees. If you want employees to run, not walk to their next review period, create an aggressive raise program to engage and reward them. This will help increase productivity and reduce turnover, training costs, and errors. The bottom line for management is that above-average employee costs are less than the costs of below-average employees.

Chapter 7

Management Skills Tune-Up

Now you know the secret to motivating and retaining your best employees. Before you get started, it's important you do a management skills tune-up. The 5-Step Performance Compensation Program doesn't replace good management techniques; it works in conjunction with them. Managing requires a variety of skills necessary to deal with all the activities and people involved. Meeting the day-to-day demands can be challenging if you lack the knowledge or experience. Below are fundamental management activities with some best practices and tips.

1. Recruiting
2. Interviewing
3. Hiring
4. Training
5. Budgeting
6. Staffing
7. Scheduling
8. Coaching and motivating
9. Corrective action
10. Reviews
11. Promoting
12. Payroll

13. Reporting
14. Planning / Organization
15. Quality Control / Call Monitoring

Recruiting

Recruiting procedures attract prospective employees to your department or company. Use a positive and upbeat approach when describing your company's story and history. Include your own story and what attracted you to the company. Candidates will see opportunities when they know where the company has been and where it's going. Explain the specific job functions they're applying for and stress the positive aspects of the job (e.g., training, advancement, shifts, and benefits). Telling them the difficult aspects of the job as well will give you credibility and weed out individuals who aren't up for the challenge. Here's an example of a recruiting script:

Sample Recruiting Script

The company has been a leader in the industry for X number of years. We distribute several different product lines in a number of states and have X number of store locations. These product lines include X, Y, and Z. The customer service representatives answer calls and place orders on the computer.

The position you're applying for is a heavy call volume and data entry position. Benefits include medical, dental, vision, a 401K plan with X percent matched, direct deposit, seven paid holidays, two weeks paid vacation, one week paid sick, bereavement for family members, paid jury duty, employee purchase discount, a wellness plan, a stop smoking assistance program, and amusement park discounts.

Hours of operation are Monday through Friday, 7:00 AM to 5:00 PM, the dress code is business casual, pay days are every other Friday, and drug screening is required for all job offers.

We offer an aggressive personal development and raise schedule for above-average performance.

Interviewing

Interviewing procedures help you determine whether a candidate has the skills necessary to perform a specific job function. Ask specific questions related to the job description and skill requirements. Review the company history, job duties, performance expectations, and benefits before asking your questions. This gives the applicant a chance to relax and helps answer some of the questions he or she may have. This will also reinforce the benefits of working for the company and may even make the applicant want the position more than you want them. I suggest asking questions in a non-threatening manner; this relaxes applicants and allows them to respond honestly.

Interviewing Tips

Two types of questions should *not* be asked during an interview. The first type is personal questions, such as those regarding age, race, and religion. You can avoid asking these questions by focusing on those that apply to the job description, duties, and responsibilities. The second type is closed-ended questions that can be answered with a simple yes or no reply. These questions begin with words such as "do," "have," or "will you."

Open-ended questions are the best type to ask during an interview. These questions require the applicant to think and require a more complete response. Begin your questions with words like "what," "how," and "why." Listen carefully to the answers and take notes to review later. Acknowledge the answers with a simple affirmative head movement and try not to react to silly or bad answers. Ask follow-up questions when the applicant's answers are unclear. Repeat the question if the answer doesn't correspond to your original question.

Standard Open-Ended Questions to Ask

1. What sales training have you had?
2. What are you most proud of in your career?
3. What is the one thing you've done that you wish you had done differently?
4. What did you like most and least about your last or current position?
5. If you were the owner or president of the company where you last worked, what is the one thing you would've changed?
6. What are your short- and long-term goals?
7. How do you deal with stressful situations?
8. Is there anything that would prevent you from being able to work Monday through Friday from 8:00 AM to 5:00 PM?
9. Why are you the most qualified candidate for this position?
10. What will your references say about you when we call them? In what area do you need to improve?
11. Why do you want to work here?
12. What do you think your biggest challenge would be working here?
13. How do you like to be managed?
14. Do you have any questions about the company or industry or me?

Role-playing Questions to Ask

1. How would you answer the telephone here?
2. How would you respond to a customer who has a complaint?
3. How do you resolve irate customer situations?
4. What would you say to a customer to offer an add-on sale?

Questions to Ask Supervisor and Manager Applicants

1. What should be discussed during recruiting?
2. What are some examples of questions you should and shouldn't ask during an interview?
3. Should the hiring process be easy or hard?
4. How does call monitoring help in training?
5. What are some of the challenges poor scheduling creates?
6. How can coaching be motivating?
7. What is the purpose of any corrective action?
8. How would you respond to an employee who doesn't agree with your review?
9. How do you decide between equally qualified candidates for promotion?
10. What type of work should never be delegated?
11. What are reports good for?
12. What are you most proud of in your career?
13. What do you wish you had done differently?
14. What will your references say about you?
15. What will your references say you need to improve?
16. What are your short- and long-term goals?
17. Do you have any questions for me?

Taking notes helps remind you of things you noticed during the interview process and can be used to decide between equally qualified applicants. Characteristics you may notice include confidence, attitude, nervousness, tardiness, dress, eye contact, inconsistent answers, sincerity, and honesty.

Hiring

Hiring is the process of selecting the best possible candidate and making a formal job offer. These offers are usually contingent upon passing drug screening, background, and credit checks. Be enthusiastic and realistic when making a job offer. Good applicants have choices and will take the best opportunity over the best offer. All applicants are looking for a job; however, not all are looking to work. Discuss performance expectations in depth to eliminate candidates who view "work" as just another four-letter word to avoid. As my brother says, "Hire hard and manage easy." In other words, management is easier when you're selective in your hiring process. Hiring someone with questionable ability or work experience is a gamble that usually doesn't pay off. Taking the time to consider candidates carefully will save you even more time later.

Training

Training procedures explain all the core activities for a specific function. New employees must learn the basics of every company, or what I refer to as all the "Ps." As mentioned earlier, these include the policies, procedures, programs, people, products, prices, and promotions. The learning curve can vary depending upon the company size and the number of products and services it offers. Create a training curriculum, materials, and tests to evaluate the trainee's retention. Training is a repetitive process of drill, repeat, and review.

The size of your organization will determine what kind of trainer you can afford. They can be full- or part-time trainers, leads, supervisors, managers, or even the owner of a small company. Trainers need time, knowledge, and patience to be effective. Good trainers are worth their weight in gold because what they produce will have an impact on your department and company for years. The trainer position is an excellent personal development opportunity for your employees. The 5-Step Performance Compensation Program helps reduce your training requirements by reducing your turnover.

Budgeting

Budgeting procedures forecast department revenue and costs over a twelve-month period. Department budgets are done after the sales and marketing forecasts are completed. These forecasts depend on where the industry is in its maturity cycle and how the company is positioning itself. Is the industry in the early or mature market stage? Is the company expanding by acquisition or unique marketing efforts? The early stage is difficult to anticipate and forecast. The middle stage provides sales history to help predict future trends. The mature stage provides lots of sales history for forecasting and budgeting purposes. Company growth depends on the company's financial strength and risk acceptance. Financial strength gives a company the ability to expand, and risk acceptance gives it the willingness to expand. Focus your attention on your biggest expenses, which are normally labor or material costs. Next, look at benefits, rent, telephone, and office supplies.

Staffing

Staffing procedures identify the correct number of employees required to perform the core functions and any special assignments while meeting company objectives or standards. Knowing the average daily sales and average employee productivity is essential in this process. Simply divide the daily sales forecast by the average employee productivity and add 10 percent for absenteeism. This will give the number of full-time equivalent employees required. Other types of measurements can be used, such as orders per hour, calls per hour, talk time, and hold time. Here's one example (see chapter 2 for additional examples):

Sample Formula to Determine Staffing for a Call Center

- Divide 60 minutes per hour by average talk time of 5 minutes. That equals an average productivity of 12 calls per hour.
- Divide your highest call volume per hour by the average productivity (12) to get your base staff level. For example, 200 calls per hour divided by 12 gives you 16.7 agents.
- Add 10 percent for normal vacation and sick absenteeism, or 1.7 agents per day. This means you will need a minimum of 18 agents to handle your busiest hour.
- Note that hold time standards, call flow variations, and seating restrictions also play a part in your calculations.

Factors that Influence Staffing Requirements

- **Seasonal.** Some companies do the majority of their business during the holidays (e.g., Christmas, Easter,

Independence Day, and Thanksgiving). This may require part-time or temporary staffing to handle the increase in business leading up to and including these events.

- **Product Introduction.** Some product introductions can increase business dramatically. Forecasting these changes is usually based upon sales projections. Actual sales of the products should be followed closely from the start and staffing changes made accordingly. Anticipate decreasing sales after the initial product introduction.
- **Promotional.** Coordinate staffing with marketing schedules.
- **Television Advertisement**. Television advertisements generate immediate response from customers and necessitate staffing requirements. Use historical data whenever available, adjusting for market penetration to help forecast your staffing needs. Adjust staffing as needed based upon actual results.
- **Print Advertisement.** Customer response can vary depending on the frequency of the print advertisement (daily, weekly, or monthly). Other considerations include the type of print advertisement:
  o *Immediate*—delivery of catalogs
  o *Prior to holiday*—seasonal catalogs
  o *Period of time*—monthly or bi-monthly catalogs
  o *Limited offer*—while supplies last
- **Internet Advertisement**. Requires additional staffing.
- **Shipping Cut-off Times**. Spikes in activity are expected to increase prior to the shipping cut-off times for your company.
- **Times of the Day**. Hourly variations are based upon your customers' business flow, hours of operation, time zones, and their slow time when they have time to order.
- **Days of the Week**. Daily variations are based upon your customers' business flow, the days they are closed, and days they need delivery.
- **Month End**. Sales activity increases at the end of the month or commission period.

Scheduling

Scheduling procedures match business needs with staffing requirements. Proper scheduling minimizes labor costs and maximizes service levels. You can minimize overtime and idle time with proper scheduling. Divide average work required per hour by the average employee productivity per hour in scheduling. Try to keep your schedule as simple as possible (e.g., Monday through Friday, 8:00 AM to 5:00 PM). Companies that operate with longer or variable hours will require more complicated scheduling. Rotating schedules may be required to handle various shifts, weekends, or holidays. The twenty-four-hours-per-day and 365-days-per-year schedules are the most challenging. Businesses of all sizes have scheduling challenges. Small companies have fewer employees to cover all shifts and absences due to vacation or sickness. Medium-sized companies have higher labor costs during off-peak hours. This hurts productivity and adds pressure to reduce staff during seasonal fluctuations. Large companies have more resources to invest in scheduling analysis and programs. This investment usually pays for itself with ongoing labor cost savings.

Spreadsheets are a flexible scheduling tool, which can be easily modified. You can keep track of schedules, days off, breaks, lunches, hours, extensions, location, assignments, hire dates, birthdays, etc.

Name	Hours	OFF	Break 1	Lunch	Break 2	Hrs	Ext.	Loc	Title	Hire	B-day
Amy	7a-12p	6,7	9a	NA	11a	25	3	103	CSR	3/19/02	12/27
Andy	7a-3:30p	6,7	9a	11a	2p	40	2	105	CSR	8/19/02	9/10
Ann	7a-3:30p	6,7	9a	12p	2p	40	1	104	CSR	10/27/03	10/7
Bill	8:30a-5p	6,7	10:45a	1:30p	3:45p	39	6	109	CSR	8/28/06	7/4
Bob	8a-4:30p	6,7	10:30a	1p	3:45p	40	4	125	CSR	2/19/07	2/1
Bonnie	8:30a-5p	6,7	10:45a	1:30p	3:45p	40	5	108	Reception	2/26/07	6/5
Cathy	8:30a-3:30p	6,7	10:30a	12:30p	NA	32	7	107	CSR	3/19/07	1/9
Connie	8:30a-5p	6,7	10:45a	1:30p	3:45p	40	8	110	Supervisor	4/30/07	9/30
Danielle	9:30a-5p	6,7	10:15a	12:30p	3:15p	35	11	131	CSR	1/16/06	11/10
David	8a-3:30p	6,7	10a	12p	2:30p	35	10	122	CSR	9/26/05	4/20
Dawn	7:45a-4:15p	6,7	11a	12p	1p	40	9	102	CSR	4/3/06	2/8
Edward	9:30a-5p	6,7	11:30a	1:30p	3:45p	35	12	132	CSR	9/8/03	12/11
Emily	8a-4:30p	6,7	10a	12p	2:30p	40	13	126	Supervisor	6/26/06	7/7
Faye	8a-4:30p	6,7	9:45a	12p	2:30p	40	15	127	CSR	11/16/06	2/3
Frank	9a-2:30p	6,7	11a	NA	1p	28	14	134	CSR	7/10/06	4/7

Harold	9a-5p	6,7	10:15a	1p	3:15p	35	16	137	CSR	12/15/03	5/6
Irene	8:30a-5p	6,7	10:15a	12:30p	3:15p	40	17	111	CSR	7/24/06	3/6
Jack	9:30a-5p	6,7	10:30a	1p	3:30p	37	18	133	CSR	10/11/04	8/22
Jennifer	8a-4:30p	6,7	10a	12p	2:30p	40	20	128	CSR	6/21/04	7/25
Jessica	8a-3:30p	6,7	10a	12:30p	2:30p	35	19	123	CSR	3/12/07	1/2
Karen	8:30a-5p	6,7	10:30a	1p	3:30p	40	22	113	CSR	3/12/07	8/3
Kim	8:30a-5p	6,7	10:30a	1p	3:30p	40	21	112	Manager	6/14/04	7/22
Larry	9a-2p	6,7	11a	NA	1p	25	23	135	CSR	11/14/05	8/22
Leslie	8:30a-5p	6,7	10:30a	1p	3:30p	37	26	114	CSR	12/19/05	6/14
Lisa	8a-5p	6,7	10a	12p	3p	40	25	130	Trainer	5/3/99	2/5
Lynn	8a-4:30p	6,7	10:15a	12:30p	2:15p	40	24	129	CSR	4/30/07	11/29
Mary	8a-3:30p	6,7	9:30a	12:30p	2:30p	35	27	124	CSR	7/8/96	4/12
Melissa	8:30a-5p	6,7	10:15a	12:30p	3:15p	40	28	115	CSR	7/14/03	10/5
Nancy	7a-3:30p	6,7	9a	12p	1:45p	40	29	106	CSR	12/27/05	9/22
Nick	9a-4:30p	6,7	10:45a	1p	2:45p	35	30	136	CSR	6/7/04	10/29
Sally	8:450a-2:30p	5,6,7	11a	NA	1p	23	34	120	CSR	1/9/06	2/24
Sam	7:30a-3p	6,7	10a	NA	NA	35	31	101	CSR	7/17/06	9/2
Sarah	8:30a-5p	6,7	10:30a	1p	3:30p	40	33	116	CSR	3/26/07	8/17
Shawn	8:45a-1:45p	6,7	11a	NA	1p	25	32	121	CSR	11/7/05	10/22
Vickie	8:30a-5p	6,7	10:30a	1p	3:30p	40	35	117	Lead	1/22/07	8/1

Coaching and Motivating

Coaching encourages and motivates employees to try their best. Recognition is the easiest and most effective way to motivate employees. Try to catch your employees doing the right things. You'll be surprised how much harder employees will work for recognition. Using the 6-Step Performance Development Meeting or PDM format will motivate the employee to keep trying their best.

6-Step Performance Development Meeting

1. Ask questions about the employee's personal interests (e.g., kids, family, dogs, house, car, and vacation).
2. Tell them what you like best about them (e.g., "I like your positive attitude.").
3. Ask them what they think their biggest strength on the job is. Wait for a response.
4. Ask them what area they think they could improve on the job. Agree if appropriate.

5. Tell them what areas they need to improve on the job. Use one suggestion at a time.

6. Ask for their commitment to improve in this area (e.g., "Do I have your commitment in this area?").

The Performance Development Format is the best management technique I have seen in years. You start each meeting by asking a question about something that's important to the employee. Don't get too personal; just show interest in what matters to the employee. This step is critical and should be done before discussing what's important to you and the company.

Sample Coaching Conversation using the Performance Development Format

(Personal interests)
Supervisor: How's the family, Bob?
Employee: Fine.
Supervisor: What are your plans for the weekend?
Employee: Just the Honey-do list.
Supervisor: I know what you mean. I've got one of those too. What do you look forward to the most on your days off?
Employee: Playing with the kids.
Supervisor: How old are they now?
Employee: Megan is three, and Josh is six years old.
Supervisor: What games do they like to play?
Employee: Megan likes playing house, and Josh likes basketball.
Supervisor: Kids are so cute at those ages.

(What you like best about the employee)
Supervisor: It's great to have this chance to meet with you, Bob. The thing I like best about you is you're always on time for work and ready to go when your shift begins.

(What the employee thinks his or her strength is)
Supervisor: Let me ask you, Bob, what do you think one of your biggest strengths is?
Employee: My productivity is always above average.
Supervisor: I agree. You do maintain a high level of productivity.

(What the employee thinks he or she could improve)
Supervisor: What is an area you could improve?
Employee: My sales are not where I would like them to be.
Supervisor: I agree with you, Bob.

(What you wanted to coach the employee on)
Supervisor: Your sales numbers are what I wanted to discuss with you and see how you could improve. Why do you think your sales are below average, Bob?
Employee: I forget to offer the promotions to each customer.
Supervisor: I noticed that on some of your calls I monitored. Do you have an idea about how you could remember to make an offer to every customer?
Employee: I was thinking of making a sign and sticking it on my computer monitor to remind me.
Supervisor: That's a great idea, Bob.

(Getting employee commitment)
Supervisor: So Bob, I have your commitment that you're going to post a reminder on your monitor to offer every customer a promotion?
Employee: Yes.
Supervisor: Great. I know that's helped other agents in the past. I look forward to our next meeting to see how that helped your sales. Have a great weekend with the kids

Corrective Action

Corrective action makes employees aware of what they're doing wrong and what is expected of them. Employees need to be made aware of issues as soon as possible. Using the 6-Step Performance Development Meeting or PDM format will make it a more positive experience. Here's how the conversation would flow:

Sample Corrective Action Conversation using the Performance Development Format

(Personal interests)
Supervisor: How are the kids, Jane?
Employee: Sick.
Supervisor: Are both of them sick?
Employee: Yes.

Supervisor: I know how tough that can be. My oldest daughter still helps me out with her little brother. How old are they now?
Employee: Jean is twelve, and Joey is six.
Supervisor: They grow so fast.

(What you like best about the employee)
Supervisor: It's great to have this chance to meet with you, Jane. The thing I like best about you is you're always so friendly and helpful with the customers.

(What the employee thinks his or her strength is)
Supervisor: Let me ask you, Jane, what do you think one of your biggest strengths is?
Employee: My sales are always above average.
Supervisor: I agree. You do maintain a high level of sales.

(What the employee thinks he or she could improve)
Supervisor: What is an area you could improve?
Employee: My tardiness could be better.
Supervisor: I agree with you, Jane.

(What you wanted to counsel the employee on)
Supervisor: Your tardiness is what I wanted to discuss with you and see how you could improve. Do you have any ideas about how you could improve your tardiness?
Employee: It's very hard to get the kids up in the morning.
Supervisor: I know what you mean. Would changing you to a later shift help?
Employee: I really like my current shift and don't want to change.
Supervisor: What could you do to make sure you're on time every day?
Employee: I'm going to get the kids in bed earlier at night.
Supervisor: That's a great idea, Jane.

(Getting employee commitment)
Supervisor: So, Jane, I have your commitment that you're going to be on time every day?
Employee: Yes.
Supervisor: Great, so we'll keep you on your current shift for now. I look forward to our next meeting to hear how your plan of getting the kids to bed worked. Hope the kids feel better soon.

Here's a tip: Do your least favorite thing first, and the rest of your day will go better. When you put off doing your least favorite tasks until the end of the day, they become a worry or burden that hampers your productivity until they're completed. I adopted this idea from Zig Ziglar's *See You at the Top* training years ago. Managers usually conduct their coaching from best to worst. Turn that around: do the worst first and save the best for last. What you'll find is that the worst coaching doesn't go as badly as you thought it would. You'll find that the lowest performers know who they are and what areas they need to improve. It usually goes smoother than coaching average employees who think their performance is better than the numbers show. Completing these tasks first will free your mind and help you focus and be more productive for the rest of the day.

Reviewing

Reviewing procedures evaluate an employee's performance. Track each individual's monthly performance for all important performance areas (e.g., orders placed, call monitoring scores, sales, error ratio, attendance, and quiz scores). Base your scoring against the group average. Using the 6-Step PDM format during reviews gets employees to commit to improving areas of development. Here's how the conversation would flow:

Sample Review Conversation using the Performance Development Format

(Personal interests)
Supervisor: How's your new car, Jen?
Employee: I love it.
Supervisor: What color did you get?
Employee: It's white with tan interior.
Supervisor: I love the new car smell. Are you planning any road trips?
Employee: This weekend I'm going to the desert.
Supervisor: What are you going to do there?
Employee: I want to see the flowers blossom.
Supervisor: The flowers are amazing this time of the year. That sounds like a fun trip.

(What you like best about the employee)
Supervisor: It's great to have this chance to meet with you, Jen. The thing I like best about you is you're always smiling and so friendly to everyone.

(What the employee thinks his or her strength is)
Supervisor: Let me ask you, Jen, what do you think one of your biggest strengths is?
Employee: My productivity is above average.
Supervisor: I agree. You do maintain a high level of productivity.

(What the employee thinks he or she could improve)
Supervisor: What is an area you could improve?
Employee: My call monitoring scores could be better.
Supervisor: I agree with you, Jen.

(What you wanted to review the employee on)
Supervisor: Your call monitoring is an area you could improve on your review, Jen. Do you have any ideas about how you could improve in this area?
Employee: It's hard to remember everything I'm supposed to ask or say to the customer.
Supervisor: You could focus on one thing per day. By the end of the week, you'll have all the items you keep forgetting covered.
Employee: I never thought of that.
Supervisor: Would you like me to make a list for you?
Employee: No, I can do that myself.
Supervisor: That's great, Jen.

(Getting employee commitment)
Supervisor: So Jen, I have your commitment that you're going to make a list and focus on one item per day?
Employee: Yes.
Supervisor: I look forward to our next meeting to hear how that worked for you. Enjoy your trip to the desert this weekend in your new car.

Employees don't need to have perfect performance in every category to achieve a high rating. Different performance categories can be given different weight and emphasis. What the employee says on the telephone and how they say it can be your most important performance measurement. The error rate can be given less weight because it normally decreases with time and experience.

Raises Based on Reviews

The standard practice for raises is every employee receives the same percentage increase for the same performance level. This rewards senior employees with higher hourly wages more than new employees with lower hourly wages. Here's an example: Two employees have the same average review performance. One has three years of experience and the other has one year of experience. One is paid $14.00 per hour, and the other is paid $11.00 per hour. If the budgeted increase for the company is 4 percent, then each average performance review receives a 4 percent increase. The senior employee with three years would get $.56, and the new employee would receive $.44. You end up paying more to a senior employee you expect better performance from than a newer employee. The result is lower motivation for both senior and new employees alike.

Employees with equal performance deserve an equal reward. You can accomplish this by rewarding review scores rather than the current wage. Give the same monetary increase for the same performance review score. Here's the example: Two employees with different pay levels have the same performance. The budget is 4 percent and the average department wage is $12.00. Give each average review 4 percent of the average $12.00 wage (or $.48). Rewarding performance rather than current pay levels motivates them to keep trying their best.

Promoting

Promoting procedures select an internal candidate for a position with higher responsibility. The new position may have different skill requirements. As in interviewing, create a job description including skill requirements. Prepare a list of open-ended interview questions. Base your selection primarily on the skill requirements of the new position. Past performance should be considered only for those skills that transfer to the new position (e.g., a great salesperson may not have the skills required for sales management). Customer service is not a career choice for most employees, and they will often seek advancement opportunities. Take advantage of this reality and encourage customer service agents to grow within your company. I've found customer service positions provide excellent communication skills that transfer to a wide range of business areas including accounting, management, retail, and sales.

Payroll

Payroll procedures verify regular and overtime hours worked along with holiday, vacation, sick, bereavement, jury duty, and personal time. This can be tedious and time-consuming, but it's very important you ensure sure your employees are paid correctly. It will avoid morale issues and save time in the long run. Attendance recordkeeping will also save time with your employee reviews. Closely monitor your budget versus actual payroll costs. Adjust schedules or staffing to reduce unnecessary overtime and idle time. Some businesses with seasonal fluctuations may require temporary staff additions.

Reporting

Reports provide upper management with performance statistics. Reports can be weekly, biweekly, monthly, quarterly, and annual. These reports include basic performance characteristics like calls answered, abandon rate, hold time, talk time, orders processed, sales, problem reports, call monitoring scores, error rates, staffing, turnover, and project progress reports. Tracking key indicators will reveal department performance and business trends. Trends help in scheduling, staffing, and preparing budgets for your department. Upper management usually sets each department's goals.

Planning and Organization

Planning prioritizes activities and schedules time to do those activities. Some people think planning is done only at the beginning of the year during the budget process. Proper planning helps you hire, train, and schedule enough staff to cover normal absenteeism and business spikes. Continuous planning is time well spent and necessary to handle constant changes in the business environment. Use a desk calendar and written or electronic planner to schedule your time. Take ten minutes at the beginning of each day to plan for changes on a daily, weekly, monthly, and quarterly basis. Remember the day ends as soon as it begins as far as planning is concerned. Adjustments can be made daily to deal with unforeseeable challenges or changes in the business flow. You can switch assignments when absenteeism or volume is high. You can switch to manual or paper processes when computers or telephones go down. Anyone who says they don't have time to plan is spending too much time trying to make a poor plan work.

Call Monitoring and Quality Control

Call monitoring verifies proper customer interaction by following scripts and policy and procedure. This quality control is conducted by a supervisor, manager, or specialized group. Objective categories are items that an agent either did or didn't do and are the easiest to score (e.g., "Did the agent thank the caller at the end of call?"). Subjective categories for tone and attitude usually require a recorded call that can be reviewed with an agent. Give emphasis and priority to any categories by assigning higher point values. Monitoring should be done on a regular basis. Using the 6-Step PDM format will motivate the employee to keep trying their best. Here's an example of how the conversation would flow:

Sample Motivational Conversation using the Performance Development Format

(Personal interests)
Supervisor: How's the family, Barbara?
Employee: Not so good.
Supervisor: Why is that, Barbara?
Employee: My teenager won't listen to me.
Supervisor: I know how frustrating that can be. I've got one of those too. Teenagers can be very challenging.

(What you like best about the employee)
Supervisor: It's great to have this chance to meet with you, Barbara. The thing I like best about you is you're always offering customers promotions.

(What the employee thinks his or her strength is)
Supervisor: Let me ask you, Barbara, what do you think one of your biggest strengths is?
Employee: My positive attitude.
Supervisor: I agree. You're always positive.

(What the employee thinks he or she could improve)
Supervisor: What is an area you could improve?
Employee: My sales are not where I would like them to be.
Supervisor: I agree with you, Barbara.

(What you wanted to coach the employee on)
Supervisor: Your sales are what I wanted to discuss with you and see how you could improve. Why do you think your sales aren't where you would like them to be?
Employee: Many customers don't want what I suggest to them.
Supervisor: I noticed that on some of your calls I monitored. Do you have an idea about how you could make better suggestive selling offers?
Employee: Not really.
Supervisor: I would suggest listening closer to what customers say when asking them questions.
Employee: You're right. I'm usually focused on what I want to tell the customer next.

(Getting employee commitment)
Supervisor: So, Barbara, I have your commitment that you're going to listen more closely to what the customer says?
Employee: Yes.
Supervisor: Great, I know that's helped other agents in the past. I look forward to our next meeting to see how that helped your sales. Good luck with your teenager.

Here's a tip: Knowing the challenges an employee faces in their personal life can give insight to the challenges they face on the job. Performance development meetings can seem like an opportunity to offer helpful suggestions in an employee's personal life. Try to offer only professional advice and let the employee make his or her own personal connections.

Telephone Scripts

Telephone Scripts provide consistency and a high level of customer service. The following is a simple example of a receptionist script:

Sample Script for a Telephone Receptionist

The greeting is the customer's first impression of you and sets the tone for the call.

> *Receptionist:* Thank you for calling Superior. My name is Sue. How can I help you?
> *Caller:* I would like to make an appointment.

Assurance of help lets the customer know you are the right person.

> *Receptionist:* I can certainly help with that.

The name exchange makes the call more personal and friendly.

> *Receptionist:* Again, my name is Sue. May I have your name please?
> *Caller:* My name is Tom.

Open-ended questions invite the customer to provide needed sales information.

> *Receptionist:* Tom, when would you like to come in?
> *Caller:* Tomorrow.

Clarifying and verifying will reduce confusion and firm up the appointment.

> *Receptionist:* Great. We'll see you on Wednesday the twenty-fourth at 3:00 PM.

Always thank the customer again for calling your business.
> *Receptionist:* Thanks again, Tom, for calling Superior.

Conclusion

I hope you found these management tips helpful. If you're not already using these techniques, give them a try. Don't worry about making mistakes, because practice makes perfect. Applicants and employees may not even notice you've changed anything. They will appreciate your professional and caring approach. Your employees will get better as you use these standard recruiting, interviewing, coaching, and reviewing techniques.

Now you're ready to design your own Performance Compensation Program that fits the needs of your department or company. Decide what's important and measurable for your employees' performance. Let the employees know what their goals are and post the results daily. Start new employees below the industry average wage. Reward those employees who exceed your standards with pay adjustments on a periodic basis. Continue this process until the employees' pay levels matches their performance levels. Your job will get easier when all of your employees know you're trying to catch them exceeding your expectations.

Combining the 5-Step Performance Compensation Program with good management practices is hard to beat. It will be hard for your employees to find another company that appreciates their efforts more than you do, it will be harder for your competition to steal your best employees from you, and it will be hard for your customers to find another company they enjoy doing business more when your employees are experienced, knowledgeable, and motivated. Best of luck as you start to turn your employee turnover around.